90 DAYS CHALLENGE

*Step-by-Step Coaching to Activate
Your Strengths for Success*

ISBN-13: 978-1508414841
ISBN-10: 150841484X

VIYA CHEN

Speaker, Author and Strengths Business Coach

The founder of VIABIZ Coaching and Consultancy based in Singapore, Viya is the first Gallup Certified Strengths Coach of Taiwan, an ACC Business Coach, a Senior Consultant, and a Business Leader on ways to improve individual, team, and organizational performance. She has more than 20 years of executive experience at Fortune 100 companies in the management, marketing, sales, research, and non-profit sectors. She has a proven track record in delivering effective multinational strategies to drive brand leadership and sustainable growth across the APMEA region.

Viya has led the Strengths 4 Success program on corporate speaking, facilitating training, and coaching for business leaders and entrepreneurs. She uses a Strengths-Based development philosophy, offering the program in Chinese and English. She regularly speaks to leadership audiences and business leaders in Asia about the importance of activating their strengths and aligning their brand vision to create a culture and brand fueled by purpose. She is a leader in brand strategy and has been quoted as an industry expert in many media and business publications. She helps clients transform their organizations to meet their most critical business needs by implementing best practices in customer and employee engagement, business strategy, strengths-based development, and brand and leadership development.

Viya most recently served as the ExCo Committee of ICF Singapore to develop the Coaching for Community initiative. She helps coaches to support leaders by activating their strengths, clarifying their purpose, and increasing their performance. She holds a Master's Degree in Marketing Communication from Michigan State University in the USA and a Global Leadership Program Certificate from Thunderbird University. She is a Gallup-certified Strengths coach, ACC, ACTP, ACTA. Her personal mission is to be a catalyst for inspiring leaders to transform their organizations and build a platform to support coaches to see and fulfill their dream of impacting the world.

www.StrengthsBusiness.com

CONTENTS

PREFACE

90 DAYS TO ACTIVATE YOUR STRENGTHS FOR SUCCESS

Everyone needs a vision to know how to activate their strengths in order to fulfill their dream. Without an awareness of your strengths, it's almost impossible for you to lead effectively. Explore and reflect the purpose of your business and your life by learning and knowing your strengths:

- What are your innate talents and strengths?

- Do you have any unrealized ambitions?

- Are you ready to embrace change?

- Are you longing for the prospects that could occur over the next ten years?

- Are you resolved to create an optimistic future and get started by taking action?

- Are you ready to lead yourself or your team by using the power of strengths?

- Do you want to create and fulfill your vision?

- Do you wonder how your strengths can guarantee your future?

- How does a strengths-driven life work? What is its objective?

This workbook will help you take the 90-day challenge to unlock your power and activate your strengths for success. You will be able to make the most out of your talents, maximize your potential and create visions, and define the future as you picture it. This will encourage you to take steps toward your future wholeheartedly.

UNLOCK THE POWER — ACTIVATE STRENGTHS FOR SUCCESS

If you cannot describe the process you are following, you don't know what you are doing. Multinational companies generally have a good business system to help employees effectively manage large-scale operations that involve thousands of employees. Many of us know how to activate or support the system but may not know how to put our own life or business into the right structure or positioning.

Some entrepreneurs or SME owners do business but lack a proper business system. This may be due to the business owner's ignorance, or it may be simply due to the fact that they are unaware of their strengths. The first step in activating your journey from Strengths to Success is to become aware of and visualize your strengths. Let us think about the following questions:

1. What's the purpose of your life?

2. What are your Strengths?

3. What does your future look like?

4. What's your SHAPE?

INVEST IN YOUR SHAPE

SHAPE stands for the five principles that will unwrap your inherited gift and redeem the lifestyle you have always dreamed of. Write down your SHAPE and visualize what these principles look like. This will help you work toward your success by articulating who you are and what your ultimate goal in life is.

The inventory list of five principals that you already have include:

1. Strengths – Become aware of your strengths

2. Heart – Listen to your heart

3. Abilities – Discover your abilities

4. Personality – Stay true to your personality

5. Experience – Appreciate your experience

Knowing your SHAPE, visualizing it, and motivating yourself will be the best way to maximize your ability to consistently produce positive outcomes. During this program, you will learn how to integrate the principles of strengths-based development into your business and improve your life by:

- Having a better understanding of your talents and how to use them to produce results and reach your goals

- Applying your greatest talents to your role and integrating your strengths to become a more effective person so you're able to enjoy your life with freedom

- Exploring the opportunity to overcome obstacles, weaknesses, and vulnerabilities

- Knowing how to use your strengths to transform your relationships

- Understanding your unique strengths within the context of others

- Providing techniques for using strengths-based development to address specific team-related issues and challenges

- Helping you to discover, develop, and use your unique talents for greater team engagement and productivity

BECOME AWARE OF YOUR STRENGTHS

Do you know what your strengths are? Certainly you were informed of what they were while you were in school. You made an excellent grade on this test, and therefore you are good at that subject. However, oftentimes good grades don't actually reveal your true strengths, and bad grades don't reflect a true measurement of your intelligence.

Have you ever known someone who excelled in school but failed at life? On the opposite side of that coin, have you known someone who failed in school but excelled at life? Of course you do. Some of the wealthiest, most successful entrepreneurs, inventors and entertainers failed in school. How did they discover their strengths, despite being repeatedly told that they're a failure?

There's an old saying: "Necessity is the mother of invention." Some poor students find the ingenuity necessary to maneuver around their bad grades and discover their own, unconventional path. Whether or not you believe it was true, the possibility that Albert Einstein was a bad student has persisted for generations for several reasons.

One reason is that grading systems have long been considered inaccurate, and they're subsequently being constantly reevaluated. As recently as the 1980s, there were smart, middle and dumb classes in many cultures. This horrible reality was wisely deemed biased and archaic. Can you imagine the possibility that Albert Einstein was relegated to a dumb class?

Another reason for Einstein's story being told is that regardless of what you're informed of about yourself or who's telling you, you can ignore it and be the brilliant person you truly are by discovering and capitalizing on your strengths.

LISTEN TO YOUR HEART

An old showtune is frequently belted during cabaret acts across the globe: "You gotta have heart." Other anthems have been remade numerous times: "Follow your heart." More recent songs convey a different notion: "Listen to your heart."

A little passion can go a long way. Have you ever met someone and felt like your hair flew back due to the sheer confidence they exuded? These kinds of people believe in themselves and their value to the point that they don't even see the possibility of failure. Success is the only option.

A lot of variables factor into being a successful salesperson, but one of them is certainly being passionate about the product you're selling. Even someone who's poor at sales by nature can sell a product they believe in.

When reflecting on being in a situation where they were surrounded by peer pressure and had to make a choice, many people say, "I just knew it wasn't right." This is a different way of interpreting the use of the word heart-gumption.

Gumption is closely related to common sense. Sometimes you can get so wrapped up in a situation or a project that you can lose sight of what you innately know to be true. You've painstakingly memorized so many details about a subject, you can't see the big picture. If you take a step back and remember your common sense, you can see solutions to problems that you may have overlooked because all of your memorization was clouding your thinking.

DISCOVER YOUR ABILITIES

If you've ever been in a play or a musical, you'll remember the importance of casting. At some point, even watching reality television, you've seen someone audition for a role with the absolutely inaccurate notion that a role was right for them.

Part of being a successful actor is acknowledging the roles that you'll excel at. Can you imagine Jerry Lewis playing Rocky? He never would've considered auditioning for this role because he could gauge what roles he would be popular in just from reading a script.

However, this doesn't mean you should sell yourself short. Remember the old adage, "You never know unless you try." If Jerry Lewis had never auditioned for anything, he might never have discovered how internationally popular he would be playing comic roles opposite leading men like Dean Martin.

Like getting an immediate reaction from an audience, you might discover some abilities you haven't considering pursuing by asking friends, family members and colleagues what they think you'd be good at. They might see potential in you that you don't see in yourself.

Another way to figure out what it makes sense for you to pursue can be reevaluating the true nature of your personality.

STAY TRUE TO YOUR PERSONALITY

Many people pursue jobs, interests, and even romances in a rudderless or even scatterbrained way. They flail around in every direction, following whatever shiny object garners their attention. The result is that they never seek or find a clear path. Then they wonder why they haven't attained their goals or have the life and freedom they desire. Often, this lack of direction is due to pursuing something that isn't true to your personality.

Human beings have personalities while they're still in the womb. Their circumstances are altered, often dramatically, the instant they're born, and their personalities continue to be impacted as their circumstances change.

If you're raised in a specific manner and told you're supposed to be a certain type of person that conflicts with the way you actually are, you might choose to follow paths that don't have anything to do with your innate personality. For instance, perhaps your true nature is that you would be an excellent attorney. But if you were born female into a culture that has hammered into your mind that women were intended to be quiet and docile, it might never even occur to you that you should consider going to law school.

In some subcultures, what you were intended to do professionally is known as your calling. In order to discover your calling, you might have to discard certain societal restrictions that have been placed on you without your cooperation, or even your consent. In other words, sometimes you have to unearth who you really are to find out what you should pursue vocationally.

APPRECIATE YOUR EXPERIENCE

Many people have difficulty writing their own resumes because it's been so ingrained in them that bragging is a fault. However, resumes can be viewed as a celebration of your achievements. One reason why people attend anniversary celebrations is because they believe that staying with a company or another person is in and of itself an accomplishment to be duly noted.

If you choose to enjoy writing your resume because you want to celebrate your life, you can also choose to live your life like you're sharing your resume with someone. Then your confidence will flow out of you naturally without descending into bragging because you'll remember that people want to hear about who you are and what you've accomplished. This will also help you remember that if you listen and pay attention during a conversation, you can cater the way you share your accomplishments the way you cater your resume to a specific job.

Returning to the absurdity of the concept of smart and dumb classes, some people immediately dismiss others' experiences as irrelevant because they view the other person as lesser than. However, it would be difficult to find a human being on the planet who doesn't have some sort of wisdom to impart based on their unique life experience.

You might dismiss your own experience as irrelevant because your inner judge tells you it's lesser than. "I can't share the fact that I (fill in the blank) with anyone. It's too quirky. It's not cool enough. I'm a geek." However, maybe the person that holds the key to your success shares the same interest that you've deemed unworthy of leaving your living room.

And perhaps your embarrassment about your own interests corresponds with the possibility of furthering your career and realizing your true potential.

The best opportunity for people to grow, develop and even have the chance to turn their business or life around is to identify the way people most naturally think, feel and behave. The better you know yourself, the more you can apply your talents, and the greater your potential will be to consistently act with more confidence, direction and hope.

MAKING THE MOST OF YOUR TALENTS

Raw talent is uninformed and inexperienced. It tends to be more self-oriented and is often unproductive.

Mature talent is well-informed and more practiced. It tends to be more others-oriented and highly productive.

Adapting a strengths-based approach to development doesn't mean that a person can ignore his or her weaknesses. A weakness is a shortage or misapplication of talents, skills, or knowledge that causes problems for you or others. We have to deal with or manage our weaknesses.

If you are still not clear about your strengths, you can explore your strengths from different sources of assessment. Please visit https://www.gallupstrengthscenter.com to do so. You can put your own strengths in order from the top 5 or 34 Strengths provided on the website. To take Strengths for Success, log into the Gallups website and create your account with your email address and password. The assessment Gallups Strengths Finders takes approximately 30 minutes and includes questions based on your value and everyday behavior.

You will get your Strengths Insight and an Action-Planning Guide showing you how to generate self-awareness and put your ideas into action. There are examples of what your top strengths would "Sound Like" and how they can help you utilize your talents for achievement.

Real changes must begin from the inside out. This is why it is important for us to start the transformation within ourselves. External factors refer to key areas that are dependent on external conditions. When you have full control of your inner power, you will be able to open the next chapter, which is how to leverage external factors for success.

THE POWER OF VISUALIZATION

Creativity is a highly valued skill, yet learning how to develop creativity is a new concept. Creativity is a function of the right side of the brain.

Part of developing the skill of creativity is looking at possibilities. However, today a great deal of time is spent gathering data and analyzing it. This provides information in an effort to develop plans or policies and make decisions. This is moving in the direction of certainty. Before we develop the strategic actions, let's use your creativity to review the possibilities that lay ahead in your life.

Maintaining our hope for the future is difficult to do when our vision of that future is unclear or shaky.

The challenge with bigger goals and aspirations is that they are part of the unknown. You have never lived the realization of these goals, so they don't sit naturally with you. The image of your end point is not strong enough in your mind to prevent the viewing of barriers. This causes temporary blockages to seem bigger than they really are. Then it becomes easier to pay attention to the little voice in your head that says, "What if this goal is impossible? Maybe it was just never meant to be." Then you might ignore the light at the end of the tunnel due to your fear of the unknown.

Generally speaking, there are different roles in life that you might be interested in. Or you have a strong feeling that you might be able to play these roles after you know your top strengths and identify your characteristics learned from the Gallup StrengthsFinder assessment. You can also review your personal or team Strengths Grid, which is relevant to your personal or organizational top 5 strengths, including (1) Executing (2) Influencing (3) Relationship (4) Strategic Thinking.

It is not necessary to know your top strengths in every category. However, if you're aware and appreciate your strengths, you will be able to "see" how you will be able to act or behave properly. Your Strengths Grid can lead you to getting closer to your vision. Then you can find out what types of people will support you in the areas where you have weaknesses.

Remember that the purpose of visualization is to bring an intense, intentional focus on the positive potential and natural tendencies of being who you are. You will need to create a vivid future, see that you are walking in that direction, and continue to develop your most dominant talents in order to get closer to your most important goals and desired outcomes.

SPECIFYING YOUR VISION
OF THE FUTURE

Research has indicated that people with high levels of hope are much more likely to face and overcome obstacles. They're likely to rate higher on a wide range of success indicators, such as academic performance, athletic achievement, interpersonal effectiveness, mental health, and personal well-being. When you're aware that your future will change and create purposeful innovations accordingly, you will be able to open up different parts of your brain and look at your future from a different perspective.

Visualization involves using a different part of the brain. The right side of the brain is the side that we use to visualize images, ideas, and stories. The use of language is a left-brain activity. Visualizing a situation opens up the creative elements of our brain and permits us to see things in a new or different way.

The space that we create to visualize is a meditative space. The stillness of a meditative space ensures that there are no distractions and allows us to use this other part of our brain. Looking at our life in different ways supports us being able to really 'see' where we want to go.

Your self-vision connects your subconscious and conscious minds. This informs your path forward. The beauty of visualizing your vision is that it takes a purpose and starts to turn it into specific images and ideas.

The clearer the picture you create, the greater the emotion you will attach to it. Increased emotion leads to increased action. Belief in your abilities allows you to deliver the goods when the pressure is on, especially when everyone around you says you cannot do something. This process will move you closer and closer to your goals without you even being aware that this is happening.

Create your ideal life, job, performance, or situation vividly in your mind's eye. Athletes, politicians, business people, and performers the world over use visualization to increase confidence and clarity. This results in a belief in their ability to perform at the very highest level. One of the many reasons visualization works so well is that the brain cannot distinguish between actual events that have occurred and vivid creations of the mind.

You may already have a general understanding of which side of your brain is dominant. It's your default mode, and it can be defined by what the habits of your thinking processes are. Understanding how the left and right sides of the brain are working is fundamental to initiating creativity and realizing possibilities.

You may do this exercise of visualization with or without a coach's help. There are a couple of things you can do to prepare for this exercise:

(1) First you need to make sure you feel you are in a safe and trusting space.

(2) You need to remain open to what may occur when you embrace 'idea creativity'. Coming up with creative ideas leads to possibilities and new perspectives.

Some people may believe that a list of information, tools, and facts is the best way to learn new skills or to be coached. Other people need the big picture before they get the details, so they can gain a context for their new information or learning. Still others want a bit of both. A professional coach will be able to manage all styles of learning.

Some people will be very happy to express feelings and explore possibilities. Other people will want certainty, or they begin to feel uncomfortable. Both of these needs are important. Exploring possibilities should not be fearful. It should be exciting because it allows you to develop the mind, explore the possibilities to new adventures and journeys, and see things in a different way.

Create your ideal lifestyle, job, performance, or situation vividly in your mind's eye. This will increase confidence, clarity, and belief in your ability to perform at the very best level by being the best version of yourself.

You can apply some strategies when conducting a visualization exercise. All you need is your imagination, a quiet place, and a willingness to explore the power of this amazing technique.

1. BE SPECIFIC:

Imagine yourself being, doing, or having exactly what you desire. Increase the colors, sounds, tastes, and smells. Be as vivid as you can and put yourself front and center as having or doing whatever it is that you want. See yourself confidently and calmly executing the task.

2. ATTACH EMOTION:

Live with your vision and enjoy the experience. Get excited about the possibilities that lie ahead of you. You need to consistently practice to truly visualize what your future will be like.

You also need to clear your mind from worries, concerns, and fears of reaching your vision. Look at your limited resources and imagine the possibilities after leveraging them. With the fear removed, you can truly engage in this exercise and feel the joy and excitement that comes from being, having, or doing what it is that you truly want.

3. REVIEW YOUR VISION REGULARLY:

The more often you visualize yourself having the result you want, the greater your chances of achieving your goal will be because you confidence has increased. Create a theme to express your strengths and abilities, as well as what you'll be able to offer other people. More and more, you'll develop an unshakable belief that this will in fact become reality.

Some people use a vision statement or vision board. Others create an emo card to remind themselves of the goals that they would like to achieve in their lives. Another way is to develop a "headline" that articulates what you want to achieve in the future. For example, "Suzie Chen becomes CEO of the most successful marketing firm in Singapore."

Then you need to set up your milestones in different areas of interest, such as wealth, health, relationships, family, or entertainment. The more clear you are when you write down and repeat the goal you want, the more likely you'll be to achieve your goal.

4. NO BOUNDARIES:

You can go as far and as high as you wish to go with this exercise. It's all about what you'd like your end result to be. Don't think about the HOW. Focus solely on the WHAT.

During my coaching sessions, I sometimes use different tools, such as LEGO bricks, HO cards, or THEME pictures. Or I'll develop a lifeline or passion line to encourage my client to visualize their future without boundaries. It's a fun and exciting exercise because even adults will enjoy learning about themselves while playing these games.

Visualization is one of the real gems that you should incorporate into your life if you wish to make huge progress and go beyond what you thought was possible. It's free and easy to do, and it will leave you feeling positively charged and excited.

Some of the many benefits of visualization include:

- Increased confidence and self-esteem rooted in the newfound belief that you can obtain the life you want.

- Speedier achievement of goals because the visualization provides clarity. Ideally, if you can develop images and articulate descriptions, your goal will become clearer and clearer every time you focus on them.

- Discover creativity to find solutions to issues, and see the barriers fall down between you and your vision.

- The sky is the limit as to what you can do, have, and be. Keeping this limitlessness in mind will help you craft loftier goals.

- Great excitement and emotion are generated around an event or goal because it originated in your creativity.

- A regular practice will consistently bring calm to your life and allow you to repeatedly focus on your goal. You can also view this as rehearsal for a way to approach any task.

- In order to have a successful practice, you will need to find a safe zone. This is a relaxing place that you create by yourself or with coach. You can be alone in this space or with people you trust.

- This practice gets people into a state of joy because you "create" the picture of the future you would like to be in and discover ways to put yourself there.

By focusing on the end point of a journey, you develop the point of view of a helicopter. From a helicopter, you can easily see that there are many pathways to any destination. One of the differences between high-hope individuals and low-hope individuals is that people with high hopes recognize this simple fact.

Visualizing your strengths will also bring you confidence when you recognize and embrace your own uniqueness. You have your own special purpose, and you can live your life accordingly.

The coaching tool from Gallup Strengths includes two important exercises: "Theme Insights" and "Paired Up". You will learn how to focus on your dominant talents and find ways to manage or work around your lesser talents. Decades of research have shown that these primary strengths are most directly related to achieving your true potential. Your strengths can be grouped into 34 themes, and each theme comprises many talents. After you have explored your strengths, the "Paired Up" exercise will help you gain awareness and appreciation of your dominant talents and apply those talents to everyday life.

When you see who you are, you'll be able to align your Head, Heart, and Hands. This will create a sense of empowerment and generate positive energy for your life and business. This feeling of euphoria is a powerful catalyst for everyone to persevere in what they are doing. Initially, we may not have done this correctly, but with internal alignment and perseverance, we can improve our actions. When envisioning and investing in your future, success hinges on your willingness to focus your efforts and invest the time and skills necessary to generate the desired results. Leading by your vision, you will feel confidence and continue to push through boundaries in order to achieve your desired future.

TURNING STRENGTHS INTO ACTIONS: THE MIGHTY ME COACHING MODULE

B y recording your dreams and goals on paper, you set in motion the process of becoming the person you most want to be. You are able to create your future in good hands if you can align your head, heart, and hands.

A coach is a person that will help you learn how to identify your desires, explore your strengths, and overcome your fears. The coach not only makes you mentally prepared, but also focuses on the next steps toward building your effective actions and fulfilling your dream. Here is the coaching module, including the three dimensions and three phases that I use to support my clients to become an effective leader in their business and their life:

Three Dimensions that Contribute to Coaching Strengths for Success:

(1) MULTIPLE TALENTS:

The coach helps the client become aware of their multiple talents. This process is a mustering of their strengths. The coach is creating a safe space to help clients learn their inherited talents and appreciate their best selves.

(2) INSPIRE CREATIVITY:

The coach uses Visualization and Imagination tools to unlock clients' desires, map their future, and envision their goal.

(3) GO FOR ACTION:

After clients have developed self-awareness and feel empowered by their vision, the coach will guide them through the process of creating milestones and focusing on smart goals. During this transformative journey, the coach acknowledges the plan, holds clients accountable to it, and sets up a time or means to follow up.

THREE PHASES OF COACHING STRENGTHS FOR SUCCESS:

(1) HONORING POTENTIALS:

In this phase, clients will recognize their innate talents, unique personalities, and learning characteristics. The coach is able to appreciate clients' individualization and provide the clearest understanding of themselves to create the needed emotional engagement.

(2) TRANSFORMING PERSPECTIVES:

The coach helps clients to invest in talents and turns them into mature strengths. Clients will also learn how to reframe and shift perspectives, which will create positive energy and alignment with their purpose and value.

(3) YIELDING POSSIBILITIES:

During this phase, the coach uses powerful questions and active listening to unfold the possibilities of putting change into action. The coach will help the client by unravelling barriers, celebrating possibilities, and making them feel empowered through the alignment between their Head, Heart and Guts.

EMPOWERING THE LAW
OF ATTRACTION

The Mighty Me model's law of attraction is to consciously visualize strengths and envision goals. The model will inspire clients to see who they are and picture the pathways to creating the future they can possess. Their visualization will transform into reality.

The clients will be inspired by experiencing the meditative journey of reviewing the logical thinking of the Head, the emotional feeling from the Heart, and the intention triggered by the Guts. After practicing with the left and right sides of their brain, clients will follow the enthusiasm from the alignment of their head, heart, and guts. And they will feel empowered from envisioning their goals.

Empowerment is the sense that you can integrate external power with internal power. Janet O. Hagberg has identified different stages of personal power in her book *Real Power*. We are on a continuous journey from being powerless to being powerful. The hallmark of the first stages of Real Power is the capacity to know and use your skills, take risks, act, and make things happen. This power comes from the outside. It is external power.

The first three stages of External Power are:

(1) Powerlessness
(2) Power by Association
(3) Power by Achievement

Internal Power comes from the inside. The remaining stages are based in Internal Power. They are:

(4) Power by Reflection
(5) Power by Purpose
(6) Power by Wisdom

When we activate internal power, we are no longer limited by our own minds and imaginations. We are moving to our true passion and the courage to make significant changes to our life. People find deep meaning and exude wisdom by shifting their perspective from feeling demotivated to being motivated.

The role of a coach is to motivate people to improve their performance. However, we need to be aware that motivation is not one-size-fits-all. Each individual has a unique and distinct motivational type. Everyone is motivated differently because they are at different stages regarding the power in their life. What motivates one person can demotivate another. There is no single motivational type that is better than any other. When you are working on a achieving a goal, people will be empowered by knowing where the goal comes from. After completing this process, you will:

(1) Know what is influencing your business or life

(2) Know what you believe about your abilities

(3) Know what triggers you to embrace the potential for change

(4) Set up the right environment and support system

(5) Use triggers to tap into your unconscious belief and internal power

The other way to make people feel empowered is through the technique of 'playing', which creatively opens people's minds to other possibilities. If change is key to success in life and visualization is the door to empower strengths, then the next question is how one could create a coaching atmosphere that is conducive to visualizing possibilities and turning people into players.

The most effective way of opening up these possibilities is to think about what the future looks like. It's personal, engaging, and interactive. It is filled with light, color, smell, and sound. Something that a coaching process can do is create a personal and relaxing atmosphere. This includes:

- Allocating significant time, in which clients are explicitly encouraged to talk about their dreams and their future

- Creating or giving others a support system that is conducive to sharing their goals in their business or life

- Developing some playing, visionary, visual, or game tools to inspire clients to create a story about their future.

Another simple strategy for helping people reframe a particular perspective is active listening. The natural act of providing a space where a client can be really listened to is often enough for them to explore the perspectives that lie underneath their actions. When the coach can offer a non-judgmental space, they can help the client value their strengths, find support, and feel empowered by their decision.

Any commenting will run the risk of demotivating clients. This especially includes suggesting the others "live my values not your own". We should trust the coaching processes and believe that everyones are the experts in their own lives. By providing a trusting space and really listening, you will be able to explore the countless perspectives of the potential, inspire empowerment, and lead the actions to accomplish the goals.

Strengths-based methods are a strategy for motivating and valuing our stories as they develop. You can continue to reflect on the strategies that were just detailed by answering the motivating questions that follow.

Let's begin the 90-Day Challenge to active your Strengths to Success. Ready? Let's Go!!

PART I:

EXPLORE

DISCOVER, APPRECIATE, AND INVEST IN A STRENGTHS PROFILE

A person's talents – those strengths, feelings, and behaviors that come naturally – are the source of your true potential and power. By end of this 1st part of the 'Strengths for Success" journey, you will be able to understand and start to harness your talents. The better you can apply your dominant talents, the greater potential you will have to consistently act with confidences, direction, and hope.

Thinking back over your life, what talents or strengths have always

come naturally to you?

_____

_____

_____

_____

_____

_____

_____

_____

_____

_____

_____

Let's make a list of the top 5 most important talents you can leverage.

1. _____

2. _____

3. _____

4. _____

5. _____

Which ones generates the most positive feedback from others?

_____

_____

_____

_____

_____

Do you wish you had more specific talents? What would you do

more of if you could?

_____

_____

_____

_____

_____

_____

Do you spend your time and effort focusing on your own special strengths? Do you seek to contribute your strengths to the overall mission of your organization or family?

_____

_____

_____

_____

_____

_____

Are you aware of your strengths? How do your talents influence

how you think about your role in your work and personal life?

_____

_____

_____

_____

_____

_____

Which of your talents or strengths do you wish you could use more

often? Why?

_____

_____

_____

_____

_____

_____

What was your most significant accomplishment in the past twelve

months? What do you think contributed to this success?

_____

_____

_____

_____

_____

_____

What have you learnt about yourself from your successful experience? What make you feel fulfilled and excited to get up each day for work?

_____

_____

_____

_____

_____

_____

Which activities give you the most dissatisfaction, either while you're doing them or immediately after you've finished them?

_____

_____

_____

_____

_____

_____

Think about a time when you discovered something that you do particularly well. How did your talents or strengths help you make sense of that situation? What strengths did you use or not use?

_____

_____

_____

_____

_____

_____

Sometimes our greatest talents get in the way. Which of your talents get in the way of you achieving your goal?

_____

_____

_____

_____

_____

_____

How do you think your strengths can help you to improve your performance? Describe specific ways that you could enhance your professional endeavors.

_____

_____

_____

_____

_____

_____

Where do you see connections between your talents and your

desired goals or outcomes?

_____

_____

_____

_____

_____

_____

Which people around you best support you to maximize your

strengths and achieve your goals?

_____

_____

_____

_____

_____

_____

Tell me about a time when you used one or more of your talents.

How have your talents helped you succeed in the past?

_____

_____

_____

_____

_____

_____

What have you learned about your talents? Which ones have led to

the greatest results in your personal life or at work? Could

you be utilizing your talents more often? How so?

_____

_____

_____

_____

_____

_____

How have your strengths helped you succeed in the past? How do you use these strengths in your daily life to enhance your relationships?

_____

_____

_____

_____

_____

_____

What do you struggle with that you'd like to learn more about or get better at? How will your talents help you achieve your goals? Please be specific.

_____

_____

_____

Be yourself. Use your strengths to form habits that will effectively and consistently deliver high performance. Keep an eye on strengths that might limit your effectiveness. What are some of these limiting strengths?

_____

_____

_____

_____

_____

_____

How might you use your talents to help you tackle your biggest

challenges in your work, life, or relationship?

_____

_____

_____

_____

_____

_____

If you identify your top strengths, which strength will you focus

on maximizing in the coming year and how can you use it?

Name it: THE YEAR OF _____

_____

_____

_____

_____

_____

_____

PART I:

EXPLORE: DISCOVER, APPRECIATE, AND INVEST IN A STRENGTHS PROFILE

ACTION IDEA 1:

ACTION IDEA 2:

ACTION IDEA 3:

ACTION IDEA 4:

ACTION IDEA 5:

ACTION IDEA 6:

PART II:

ENVISION

ACTIVATE AND ACCELERATE STRENGTHS THROUGH A POSITIVE APPROACH

Our greatest talents – the ways in which we most naturally think, feel, and behave – represent our innate power and potential. When we tap into this source of wisdom and power, we are more efficient; we act with more confidence, direction, and hope. Through Strengths-based coaching, a coach uses the art of asking questions and articulating opinions. This process strengthens the system as a whole, creates positive imagery through a strengths profile, and heightens your potential to help you see and fulfil your vision.

A clear and compelling vision can drive extraordinary business results. It provides a focus for people's decisions and actions, and it creates the feeling of a tribe that most people find necessary and motivating. Planning your life involves reflecting about where you want it to go. Leading your business and your life are important and need to be farsighted. Farsighted leaders take the following actions:

1. See possible futures that are good for their enterprise
2. Articulate their vision in a compelling and inclusive way
3. Model their vision
4. See past obstacles
5. Invite others to participate in their vision

You will be able to experience the Motivation Theory. In the 2nd phase of the "Strengths for Success" journey, you will explore the fundamental principal of Motivation. This theory is also called I AM Competence, which stands for:

- Inclusion – the awareness of being part of an environment

- Attitude – a predisposition may result in a positive or negative response

- Meaning – finding value in the principal

- Competence – a strong need to apply learning to the real world

You will also learn the principals of aligning your vision by doing self-coaching over the next 20 days. This process will include:

1. Motivating your mind
2. Acquiring the necessary information
3. Searching the memory
4. Triggering the memory
5. Exhibiting what you know
6. Reflecting what you have learned

You can use these principles to envision your career, wealth, and lifestyle in your mind. You can even utilize them to envision your 2nd career. Let's work together on the 2nd phase of your journey to active your vision of being successful.

The Purpose of Life

Everyone is unique. In your life journey, you must have a mission to accomplish. Please articulate what your life mission is:

_____

_____

_____

_____

_____

_____

The Core Values

Check the 10 values that you utilize most in your life:

☐ Accomplishment	☐ Fame	☐ Love
☐ Achievement	☐ Family	☐ Loyalty
☐ Advancement	☐ Freedom	☐ Order
☐ Adventure	☐ Friendship	☐ Passion
☐ Aesthetics	☐ Fulfillment	☐ Peace
☐ Affection	☐ Fun	☐ Personal Developmen
☐ Altruism	☐ Gender	☐ Physical Appearance
☐ Ancestry	☐ Generosity	☐ Pleasure
☐ Autonomy	☐ Happiness	☐ Positivity
☐ Competency	☐ Harmony	☐ Power
☐ Competitiveness	☐ Health	☐ Recognition
☐ Community	☐ Honor	☐ Relationships
☐ Control	☐ Honesty	☐ Responsibility
☐ Cooperation	☐ Humility	☐ Self-Respect
☐ Creativity	☐ Influence	☐ Serenity
☐ Culture	☐ Inner Strength	☐ Significance
☐ Dignity	☐ Integrity	☐ Skill
☐ Economic	☐ Involvement	☐ Spirituality
☐ Emotional Well-being	☐ Justice	☐ Wealth
☐ Employment	☐ Knowledge	☐ Wisdom

Now select your top five values, define what each one means to you,

and explain why:

1. _____

2. _____

3. _____

4. _____

5. _____

Picture your Future Blueprint

Where will you be in 1 year? 5 years? 10 years? What do you want to be doing? Imagine that there will be an article about you in a magazine at each point in the future. What do you want the titles to be?

1 Year: _____

5 Years: _____

10 Years: _____

The Freedom of Life

What would you do right now if money was not a concern?

If you were living that now, how would your life be different?

_____

_____

_____

_____

_____

_____

5-Year Plan

What would you learn if this type of "free" life continued for 5 years? What else do you think you need to add into your "free" life?

_____

_____

_____

_____

_____

_____

Your Passion

> What's your greatest passion right now? What makes you
> feel more in the present moment than anything else?

_____

_____

_____

_____

_____

_____

Articulate your passion further by finishing the following sentences:

- I am … _____

- I want …_____

- I will …_____

Live a Legacy

What do you want people to think about you? How do you want people to remember you? What legacy do you want to leave behind for the people you care about?

_____

_____

_____

_____

_____

_____

Check for Obstacles

Everyone encounters some obstacles when preparing for action and change. What obstacles do you currently encounter most frequently? What other obstacles do you anticipate encountering?

_____

_____

_____

_____

_____

_____

Strength that Supports You

Who can you share this personal development blueprint with? Who

will fully support you in taking action and making changes?

Who will help you overcome the obstacles you just listed?

_____

_____

_____

_____

_____

_____

Finish this sentence three times:

(1) "I am good at ..."

_____

_____

(2) "I am good at ..."

_____

_____

(3) "I am good at ..."

_____

_____

What are the goals you truly want, as opposed to the goals you think you should have or things you should be doing? If it's a SHOULD, it may be someone else's dream...

_____

_____

_____

_____

_____

_____

What would you like more of in your life right now? Is that one of your goals? Is this goal in line with your life vision and overall life plan? If you don't know, what's your gut feeling?

_____

_____

_____

_____

_____

_____

Is this goal in line with your Values? Ask yourself what's REALLY

important to you in life. Will this goal help you achieve more

of that?

_____

_____

_____

_____

_____

_____

When you think about your goal, does it give you a sense of deep contentment, 'rightness', happiness, and excitement? These are good signs that it's a healthy goal.

_____

_____

_____

_____

_____

_____

If you could have the goal RIGHT NOW, would you take it? How

does this goal fit into your life and lifestyle? Who else might

be impacted?

_____

_____

_____

_____

_____

_____

What one thing could you start doing right away to increase your

fulfillment and positively impact your work or life?

_____

_____

_____

_____

_____

_____

When you have increased your fulfilment and created a positive impact in your life, what will this look like and feel like?

_____

_____

_____

_____

_____

_____

In what area would you like to make the most impact? How would

this affect people you care about?

_____

_____

_____

_____

_____

_____

On a scale of 1 to 10, how satisfied are you with the impact you

make in your life? Why?

_____

_____

_____

_____

_____

_____

PART II:

ENVISION: ACTIVATE AND ACCELERATE STRENGTHS THROUGH A POSITIVE APPROACH

ACTION IDEA 1:

ACTION IDEA 2:

ACTION IDEA 3:

ACTION IDEA 4:

ACTION IDEA 5:

ACTION IDEA 6:

PART III:

ENGAGE

LEVERAGE COACHING QUESTIONS TO GUIDE AND SUPPORT STRENGTHS

Utilize the art and science of coaching to discover your inspirational nature, focus on creating possibilities, open dialoguqes, and live in alignment between your head, heart, and hands.

- Head: Analyze talents and awareness – Who am I? What are my potentials and my strengths?

- Heart: Explore your passion – What's my passion? Where am I going? When am I going there?

- Hands: Commit to possibilities – Why am I going in that direction? How do I sustain the changes?

What are you getting paid to do? What do you really love about

your work? Are you doing things that you shouldn't be doing?

_____

_____

_____

_____

_____

_____

What was your last peak performance?

_____

_____

_____

_____

_____

_____

What have you learned from your success?

_____

_____

_____

_____

_____

_____

What's working well? What's good about what you are currently

doing?

_____

_____

_____

_____

_____

_____

What was your most significant accomplishment in the past twelve

months? What do you think contributed to this success?

_____

_____

_____

_____

_____

_____

Using three short phrases, how would you describe yourself?

_____

_____

_____

_____

_____

_____

Of all the things you do well, which two or three do you do best?

_____

_____

_____

_____

_____

_____

What motivates you the most in your work or personal life?

_____

_____

_____

_____

_____

_____

What do you need to let go of or have more of so you can feel more fulfilled or have a greater impact? What prevents you from doing this?

_____

_____

_____

_____

_____

_____

What do you do that makes you successful? How will you keep
your attention on your intention? What is the reward?

_____

_____

_____

_____

_____

_____

How might you use your talents to help you tackle your biggest

challenges? How much energy do you have to muster to find

a solution that will overcome your challenges?

_____

_____

_____

_____

_____

_____

Do you maximize the use of your strengths to make contributions
to the organization you work for? When appropriate, do you
effectively leverage your strengths to support your colleagues?

_____

_____

_____

_____

_____

_____

List a number of contributions you could make to your organization

or in your personal life. Compare these with the contributions

you are currently making.

_____

_____

_____

_____

_____

_____

Are you attempting to understand the strengths of your colleagues,

your subordinates, and your boss? What are these strengths?

How can you utilize these strengths most effectively in

your organization?

_____

_____

_____

_____

_____

_____

What is one expectation you have for yourself right now? If you

ask your clients, colleagues, friends, or family members what

you do well, what would they say?

_____

_____

_____

_____

_____

_____

What's working well in your business and your life? What can you

do more of? What could you do differently? What would

your answer be if you had no concern about resources?

_____

_____

_____

_____

_____

_____

Where do you see the connections between your talents and your

desired outcomes?

_____

_____

_____

_____

_____

_____

What's the biggest challenge you currently face? Let's look at your

goals for the near future. What are your goals for this month?

For the next 90 days? For the next 12 months?

_____

_____

_____

_____

_____

_____

What challenges have you already tried to overcome in your

work and personal life?

_____

_____

_____

_____

_____

_____

What distractions prevent you from focusing on results and performing the best you can in your work?

_____

_____

_____

_____

_____

_____

What are some activities you would like to eliminate or reduce that are not contributing to you delivering the best performance possible?

_____

_____

_____

_____

_____

_____

When you're at your most resourceful and have the freedom to maximize your strengths, what do you think of this issue or challenge?

_____

_____

_____

_____

_____

_____

What kind of job would make you feel fulfilled and excited to get

up each day and go to work?

_____

_____

_____

_____

_____

_____

What kind of strengths would you need to have at this kind of job?

_____

_____

_____

_____

_____

_____

How have you excelled by maximizing your strengths? How can

you apply that learning to your current situation?

_____

_____

_____

_____

_____

_____

What are the good things that have happened when you've taken

action to leverage your talents or strengths?

_____

_____

_____

_____

_____

_____

What is the most important challenge you currently face? What

do you see as your greatest challenge in the future?

_____

_____

_____

_____

_____

_____

Think about your biggest challenge. What are the implications of not meeting this challenge?

_____

_____

_____

_____

_____

_____

What is the risk involved in this challenge if you do not do anything

about it?

_____

_____

_____

_____

_____

_____

What do you really want to be happening in the situation that you

are struggling through now? What have you learned about

yourself from this experience?

_____

_____

_____

_____

_____

_____

PART III:

ENGAGE: LEVERAGE COACHING QUESTIONS TO GUIDE AND SUPPORT STRENGTHS

ACTION IDEA 1:

ACTION IDEA 2:

ACTION IDEA 3:

ACTION IDEA 4:

ACTION IDEA 5:

ACTION IDEA 6:

PART IV: EMPOWER

USE STRENGTHS-BASED ACTIONS TO ACHIEVE GREATER PERFORMANCE

The inspirational nature of this 4-phase "Strengths for Success" coaching process is to discover your potential. This includes your inherited talents, strengths, personalities, and capabilities. Managing changes is a process that involves:

1. Vision and Goal Setting:	Clarify what the client needs and wants to accomplish
2. Action Plan:	Create a plan for how he or she will get there
3. Milestones:	Check and review the progress
4. Modification:	Correct courses or actions as needed
5. Celebrate Success:	Appreciate the progress the client made

This "90-Day Challenge" program combines innate talent and an analysis of strengths, allowing clients to focus on their strengths during the coaching process.

This is followed by shifting perspectives and creating possibilities. This model will explore your desires and create action plans to change. This will occur by opening dialogue and living in alignment among your Head, Heart, and Hands. Let's Take Action Now.

Can you come up with some action steps to take this week in order to make your plan happen within the next 90 days? What criteria will you use to assess the options that you will put into place in the next 90 days?

_____

_____

_____

_____

_____

_____

What will you do right now? What actions can you take to achieve

your blueprint today? What else can you accomplish within

the next week?

_____

_____

_____

_____

_____

_____

What needs to be done? Why is it important? Which of the action

items can help you achieve your goals most effectively?

_____

_____

_____

_____

_____

_____

What are other options for actions to achieve your goal in the next

90 days?

_____

_____

_____

_____

_____

_____

How can you keep your goals in sight so that you don't forget about them?

_____

_____

_____

_____

_____

_____

Who will encourage you to stay on track and help make you

feel empowered?

_____

_____

_____

_____

_____

_____

How can you overcome adversity and focus on feeling empowered every day in a way that will cause you to make progress toward accomplishing your goal?

_____

_____

_____

_____

_____

_____

How will you overcome these obstacles, including the feeling

of demotivation?

_____

_____

_____

_____

_____

_____

What's the desire outcome if you are able to turn your life or business around? How do people feel when you use your specific talents? What are they?

_____

_____

_____

_____

_____

_____

Imagine that your current challenge has been overcome. What would that feel like? How would someone who is fearless approach this challenge?

_____

_____

_____

_____

_____

_____

What can you put in place to make your goal easier to achieve?

How will you leverage your top strengths?

_____

_____

_____

_____

_____

_____

Is there any support around you that you haven't pursued that will

help you achieve your goal?

_____

_____

_____

_____

_____

_____

Create a time log of activities to determine where your time goes.

Which of the activities on your time log could be delegated to

somebody else? To whom can you delegate these activities?

_____

_____

_____

_____

_____

_____

Is there something important about achieving this goal that will

help you succeed, or that could get in the way? If you haven't

mentioned it yet, what is it?

_____

_____

_____

_____

_____

_____

What holds you back from achieving your goals? What keeps you from moving forward? How can you step up and affirm who you are?

_____

_____

_____

_____

_____

_____

Will you be able to share how you're going about achieving your

goals the next time you talk to the people you care about?

_____

_____

_____

_____

_____

_____

When you explore actions, commitment levels, and structures that may need to be in place in order to overcome potential barriers, what are they?

_____

_____

_____

_____

_____

_____

What's standing in the way of your ideal outcome if you have already leveraged your strengths?

_____

_____

_____

_____

_____

_____

Are you ready to make a commitment to achieving your goals as the result of high performance?

_____

_____

_____

_____

_____

_____

How are you going to celebrate reaching these magnificent goals?

_____

_____

_____

_____

_____

_____

PART IV:

EMPOWER: USE STRENGTHS-BASED ACTIONS TO ACHIEVE GREATER PERFORMANCE

ACTION IDEA 1:

ACTION IDEA 2:

ACTION IDEA 3:

ACTION IDEA 4:

ACTION IDEA 5:

ACTION IDEA 6:

www.ingramcontent.com/pod-product-compliance
Lightning Source LLC
Chambersburg PA
CBHW072304200526
45168CB00014B/474